Pen the ~~Hen~~

Written by Abigail Steel

Illustrated by Valentina Fontana

Pen the hen has a hat.

Peck!

Peck!

Pen pecks in the mud.

The hat tips into the mud.

Pen can go to the red hut.

The sack has a rip.

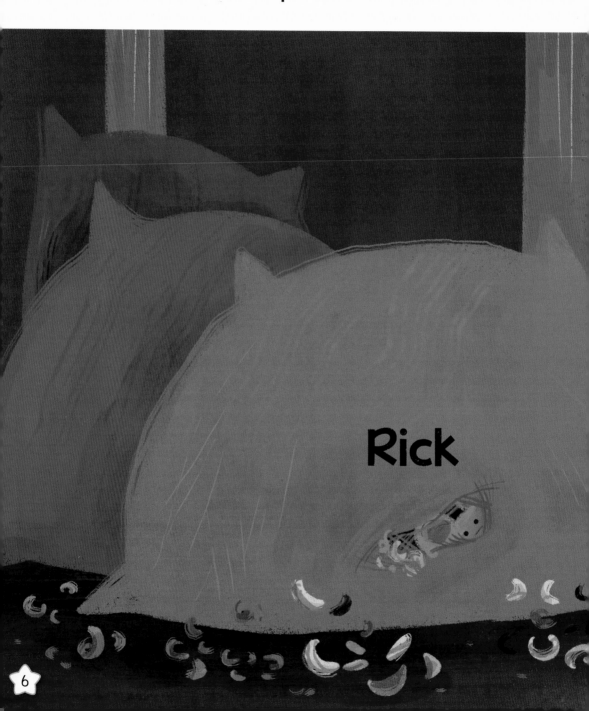

Rick

Pen pecks the sack.

Peck!
Peck!

Rick the rat pops up!

Rick gets Meg and Ed.

The rats hop up on the rock.

The rats tug to get the hat.

Talk about the story

Ask your child these questions:

1 What did Pen's hat fall into?

2 Where did Pen find Rick?

3 How many rats helped Pen?

4 How did the rats get Pen's hat back?

5 Can you think of any other animals with long tails?

6 Have you ever been to a farm? What is a farm like?

Can your child retell the story in their own words?